Presented to

_____

On the occasion of

_____

From

_____

Date

_____

SELECTIONS FROM

MY UTMOST FOR HIS HIGHEST

OSWALD CHAMBERS

BARBOUR
PUBLISHING, INC.

Published by Barbour Publishing, Inc., P.O. Box 719, Uhrichsville, Ohio 44683
http://www.barbourbooks.com

Member of the
Evangelical Christian
Publishers Association

Printed in China.

Introduction

Are we living in such human dependence upon Jesus Christ
that His life is being manifested moment by moment?

*T*he essence of Oswald Chambers's classic devotional *My Utmost
for His Highest* lies in asking the hard questions. For a man or woman
to make a true, lasting commitment to the Lord of our salvation,
Jesus Christ, much depends on honestly answering questions such as
the one above, questions that expose those worldly preservers—ego,
pride, and envy.

Selections from *My Utmost for His Highest* is a book of questions,
yes, but there are also answers. Arranged topically, this collection of
gems of inspiration and insight culled from Chambers's cherished
best-seller has a priceless purpose: to enlighten readers and enable
them to achieve the ultimate reward, eternal life.

The hard questions are only the beginning of giving—and living—
one's utmost for His highest.

Contents

ATONEMENT

"Ought not Christ to have suffered these things,
and to enter into His glory?"
Luke 24:26

*O*ur Lord's Cross is the gateway into His life. . . .

"And the LORD turned the captivity
of Job, when he prayed for his friends."
Job 42:10

I cannot make myself right with God,
I cannot make my life perfect;
I can only be right with God if I accept
the Atonement of the Lord Jesus Christ
as an absolute gift. Am I humble enough to accept it?

"In whom we have. . .the forgiveness of sins."
Ephesians 1:7

*F*orgiveness, which is so easy for us to accept, cost
the agony of Calvary. . . . When once you realize
all that it cost God to forgive you, you will be held
as in a vice, constrained by the love of God.

"Walk while ye have the light,
lest darkness come upon you."
John 12:35

Every bit of your life, physical, moral, and spiritual,
is to be judged by the standard of the Atonement.

"For by one offering he hath perfected for ever
them that are sanctified."
Hebrews 10:14

It does not matter who or what we are,
there is absolute reinstatement into God
by the death of Jesus Christ
and by no other way, not because Jesus Christ pleads,
but because He died.
It is not earned, but accepted.

BELIEF

"Believest thou this?"
John 11:26

To believe is to commit.

Belief

*"My speech and my preaching
was not with enticing words."*
1 Corinthians 2:4

Belief in Jesus is a miracle produced only
by the efficacy of Redemption,
not by impressiveness of speech, not by wooing and winning,
but by the sheer unaided power of God.

"Son of man, can these bones live?"
Ezekiel 37:3

We would far rather work for God
than believe in Him.
Am I quite sure that God will
do what I cannot do?

12

*"Whom shall I send, and who will go for us?
Then said I, Here am I; send me."*
Isaiah 6:8

Get out of your mind the idea of expecting
God to come with compulsions and pleadings.

*"I heard the voice of the Lord, saying,
Whom shall I send?"*
Isaiah 6:8

As long as I consider my personal temperament
and think about what I am fitted for,
I shall never hear the call of God.
But when I am brought into relationship with God,
I am in the condition Isaiah was in.

CHARACTER

"He went out, not knowing whither he went."
Hebrews 11:8

The final stage in the life of faith is attainment of character.

*"Take now thy son. . .and offer him there
for a burnt offering upon one of
the mountains which I will tell thee of."*
Genesis 22:2

Character determines how
a man interprets God's will (cf. Psalm 18:25–26).

*"In the year that king Uzziah died
I saw also the Lord."*
Isaiah 6:1

My vision of God depends upon
the state of my character.
Character determines revelation.

"Blessed are the pure in heart:
for they shall see God."
Matthew 5:8

Remember that vision depends on character—
the pure in heart see God.

❧

"The Lord. . .hath sent me,
that thou mightest receive thy sight."
Acts 9:17

The abiding characteristic of a spiritual man is
the interpretation of the Lord Jesus Christ
to himself, and the interpretation to others
of the purposes of God.

❧

CIRCUMSTANCES

*"And Samuel feared to shew
Eli the vision."*
1 Samuel 3:15

*G*et into the habit of saying,
"Speak, Lord,"
and life will become a romance.
Every time circumstances press, say,
"Speak, Lord"; make time to listen.

"Behold, the hour cometh. . .
that ye shall be scattered."
John 16:32

Spiritual grit
is what we need.

"Labourers together with God."
1 Corinthians 3:9

We have no right to judge where we should be put,
or to have preconceived notions as to what God is
fitting us for. God engineers everything. . . .

"All things work together for good
to them that love God."
Romans 8:28

All your circumstances are in the hands of God, therefore never think it strange concerning the circumstances you are in.

"Ye are they which have continued
with Me in My temptations."
Luke 22:28

We have the idea that we ought to shield ourselves from some of the things God brings round us. Never! God engineers circumstances and whatever they may be like we have to see that we face them while abiding continually with Him.

COMING TO CHRIST

"And when He is come,
He will convict the world of sin. . . ."
John 16:8 (RV)

It is shallow nonsense to say that God forgives us because
He is love. . . . The love of God means Calvary, and nothing less;
the love of God is spelt on the Cross
and nowhere else.

"Come unto Me."
Matthew 11:28

f I will come to Jesus my actual life will be brought into accordance with my real desires; I will actually cease from sin, and actually find the song of the Lord begin.

The attitude of coming is that the will resolutely lets go of everything and deliberately commits all to Him.

If you want to know how real you are, test yourself by these words–
"Come unto Me."

THE CROSS

"Who His own self bare
our sins in His own body on the tree."
1 Peter 2:24

The Cross was a superb triumph
in which the foundations of hell
were shaken. There is nothing more
certain in Time or Eternity
than what Jesus Christ did
on the Cross: He switched the whole
of the human race back into
a right relationship with God.

*"But God forbid that I should glory,
save in the cross of our Lord Jesus Christ."*
Galatians 6:14

*If we get away from brooding on the tragedy
of God upon the Cross in our preaching,
it produces nothing.
It does not convey the energy of God to man;
it may be interesting but it has no power.
But preach the Cross,
and the energy of God is let loose.*

23

DEPENDENCE ON GOD

"Behold, as the eyes of servants look unto the hand of their masters. . .
so our eyes wait upon the LORD our God."
Psalm 123:2

The danger is lest no longer relying on God
you ignore the lifting up of your eyes to Him.

"All my fresh springs shall be in Thee."
Psalm 87:7 (PBV)

It is the saddest thing to see people in the service of God
depending on that which the grace of God never gave them,
depending on what
they have by the accident of heredity.

"Father, I thank Thee that Thou hast heard Me."
John 11:41

Are we living in such human dependence
upon Jesus Christ that His life is being
manifested moment by moment?

25

"Will ye also go away?"
John 6:67

Live a natural life of
absolute dependence on Jesus Christ.
Never try to live the life with God
on any other line than God's line,
and that line is absolute devotion to Him.

"Lord, and what shall this man do?. . .
What is that to thee? Follow thou Me."
John 21:21–22

A saint is never consciously a saint;
a saint is consciously dependent on God.

DEVOTION

"Thomas answered and said unto Him,
My Lord and my God."
John 20:28

Are we being more devoted
to service than to Jesus Christ?

"Notwithstanding in this rejoice not,
that the spirits are subject unto you."
Luke 10:20

One life wholly devoted to God is
of more value to God than one hundred lives
simply awakened by His Spirit.

"Lovest thou me?. . . Feed My sheep."
John 21:16

People do not want to be devoted to Jesus,
but only to the cause He started. Jesus Christ
is a source of deep offence
to the educated mind of to-day
that does not want Him in any other way
than as a Comrade.

"For His name's sake they went forth."
3 John 7

The men and women Our Lord sends out on
His enterprises are the ordinary human stuff,
plus dominating devotion to Himself
wrought by the Holy Ghost.

"The Son of God, who loved me, and gave Himself for me."
Galatians 2:20

We have to battle through our moods into absolute
devotion to the Lord Jesus,
to get out of the hole-and-corner business of our experience
into abandoned devotion to Him.

DISCERNMENT

*"A conscience void of offence toward God,
and toward men."*
Acts 24:16

He does not come
with a voice like thunder;
His voice is so gentle that it is easy
to ignore it.

*"Praying always with all prayer
and supplication in the Spirit."*
Ephesians 6:18

Discernment is God's call to intercession,
never to fault finding.

❧

"If ye know these things, happy are ye if ye do them."
John 13:17

When you know you should do a thing, and do it,
immediately you know more.

❧

"The simplicity that is in Christ."
2 Corinthians 11:3

Immediately we obey, we discern.

31

DISCIPLESHIP

"Go ye therefore, and teach [disciple] all nations."
Matthew 28:19

You cannot make disciples unless
you are a disciple yourself.

"Notwithstanding in this rejoice not,
that the spirits are subject unto you."
Luke 10:20

We are not to save souls, but to disciple them.
Salvation and sanctification are the work
of God's sovereign grace;
our work as His disciples is to disciple lives
until they are wholly yielded to God.

"Lovest thou Me? . . .Feed My sheep."
John 21:16

Discipleship is based on devotion to Jesus Christ,
not on adherence to a belief or a creed.

"Thine they were, and Thou gavest them Me."
John 17:6

Our Lord makes a disciple
His own possession.

"For which of you, intending to build a tower,
sitteth not down first, and counteth the cost,
whether he have sufficient to finish it?"
Luke 14:28

Our Lord implies that the only men and women
He will use in His building enterprises
are those who love Him
personally, passionately and devotedly
beyond any of the closest ties on earth.
The conditions are stern,
but they are glorious.

FAITH

*"We have received. . .the spirit
which is of God;
that we might know the things
that are freely given to us of God."*
1 Corinthians 2:12

Faith that is sure of itself is not faith;
faith that is sure of God is the only
faith there is.

Faith

"He went out, not knowing whither he went."
Hebrews 11:8

Faith never knows where it is being led,
but it loves and knows the One Who is leading.
It is a life of faith, not of intellect and reason,
but a life of knowing Who makes us "go."
The root of faith is the knowledge of a Person,
and one of the biggest snares is the idea that
God is sure to lead us to success.

"Because thou has kept the word of My patience."
Revelation 3:10

Faith is the heroic effort of your life, you fling
yourself in reckless confidence on God.

*"And my speech and my preaching was not
with enticing words of man's wisdom, but in
demonstration of the Spirit and of power."*
I Corinthians 2:4

If your faith is in experiences, anything that
happens is likely to upset that faith;
but nothing can ever upset God or
the almighty Reality of Redemption.

"Faith as a grain of mustard seed. . . ."
Matthew 17:20

"Though He slay me, yet will I trust Him"–
this is the most sublime utterance of faith
in the whole of the Bible.

FOLLOWING JESUS

"Peter said unto Him, 'Lord,
why cannot I follow Thee now?' "
John 13:37

Never run before God's guidance.
If there is the slightest doubt, then He is not guiding.
Whenever there is doubt—don't.

"Whither I go, thou canst not follow Me now;
but thou shalt follow Me afterwards."
John 13:36

When we have come to the end of ourselves,
not in imagination but really,
we are able to receive the Holy Spirit.

GRACE

*"And whosoever shall compel
thee to go a mile,
go with him twain."*
Matthew 5:41

God does not ask us
to do the things
that are easy to us naturally;
He only asks us to do
the things
we are perfectly fitted
to do by His grace.

"Partakers of the divine nature."
2 Peter 1:4

Learn to lavish the grace
of God on others.

*"We. . .beseech you also that ye receive
not the grace of God in vain."*
2 Corinthians 6:1

The grace you had yesterday will not do for to-day.
Grace is the overflowing favour of God;
you can always reckon it is there to draw upon.

GUIDANCE

"Choose you this day whom ye will serve."
Joshua 24:15

You have no business to find out
where God is leading,
the only thing God will explain to you is Himself.

"I being in the way, the LORD led me. . . ."
Genesis 24:27

We have to be so one with God
that we do not continually
need to ask for guidance.

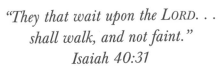

"They that wait upon the LORD. . .
shall walk, and not faint."
Isaiah 40:31

If our common-sense decisions are not His order,
He will press through them and check;
then we must be quiet and wait
for the direction of His presence.

HEARING GOD

"Yet lackest thou one thing:
sell all that thou hast. . .and come, follow Me."
Luke 18:22

Jesus Christ says a great deal that we listen to,
but do not hear; when we do hear,
His words are amazingly hard.

"Lord, I will follow Thee
whithersoever Thou goest."
Luke 9:57

The words of the Lord hurt and offend until
there is nothing left to hurt or offend.

"And they said unto Moses,
'Speak thou with us, and we will hear:
but let not God speak with us, lest we die.' "
Exodus 20:19

We show how little we love God
by preferring to listen to His servants only.
We like to listen to personal testimonies,
but we do not desire that God Himself
should speak to us.

HOLINESS

"Ye shall be holy; for I am holy."
1 Peter 1:16 (RV)

Continually restate to yourself
what the purpose of your life is.
The destined end of man
is not happiness,
nor health, but holiness.

"The friend of the bridegroom."
John 3:29

If my holiness is not drawing towards Him,
it is not holiness of the right order,
but an influence that will awaken
inordinate affection and lead souls
away into side-eddies.

"To him that overcometh. . . ."
Revelation 2:7

Holiness is the balance between my disposition
and the law of God as expressed in Jesus Christ.

HOLY SPIRIT

"For every one that asketh receiveth."
Luke 11:10

The Holy Spirit is the One Who makes real
in you all that Jesus did for you.

*"We know not what we
should pray for as we ought:
but the Spirit itself maketh intercession
for us with groanings which cannot be uttered."*
Romans 8:26

God searches your heart not to know what your
conscious prayers are, but to find out what is the prayer
of the Holy Spirit.

*"Tarry ye in the city of Jerusalem,
until ye be endued with power from on high."*
Luke 24:49

The Holy Spirit's influence and power were at work before
Pentecost, but He was not here. Immediately Our Lord
was glorified in Ascension, the Holy Spirit came into this world,
and He has been here ever since.

"Verily I say unto thee,
Thou shalt by no means come out thence,
till thou hast paid the uttermost farthing."
Matthew 5:26

God is determined to make you
pure and holy and right;
He will not allow you to escape for one moment
from the scrutiny of the Holy Spirit.

"For if we have been planted together
in the likeness of His death,
we shall be also in the likeness of His resurrection."
Romans 6:5

The Holy Spirit cannot be located as a Guest
in a house, He invades everything.

INTERCESSION

*"And the LORD turned the captivity of Job,
when he prayed for his friends."
Job 42:10*

The real business of your life
as a saved soul is intercessory prayer. . . .
Pray for your friends now;
pray for those with whom you come in contact now.

"Praying always with all prayer
and supplication in the Spirit."
Ephesians 6:18

It is impossible to intercede vitally
unless we are perfectly sure of God,
and the greatest dissipator of our relationship to
God is personal sympathy and personal prejudice.

"And He. . .wondered that
there was no intercessor."
Isaiah 59:16

Worship and intercession must go together,
the one is impossible without the other.

"Men ought always to pray,
and not to faint."
Luke 18:1

The thing to watch in intercession is
that no soul is patched up,
a soul must get through into contact
with the life of God.

"The Spirit itself maketh intercession for us
with groanings which cannot be uttered."
Romans 8:26

Get into the real work of intercession,
and remember it is a work,
a work that taxes every power;
but a work which has no snare.

INTIMACY WITH JESUS

*"This kind can come forth by nothing,
but by prayer and fasting."*
Mark 9:29

We slander God by our very eagerness
to work for Him without knowing Him.

"He calleth. . .by name."
John 10:3

The one sign of discipleship is intimate connection with Him, a knowledge of Jesus Christ which nothing can shake.

"When He had heard therefore that he was sick, He abode two days in the same place where he was."
John 11:6

If Jesus Christ is bringing you into the understanding that prayer is for the glorifying of His Father, He will give you the first sign of His intimacy–silence.

JOY

". . .so that I might finish my course
with joy, and the ministry,
which I have received
of the Lord Jesus."
Acts 20:24

Joy means the perfect fulfilment
of that for which I was created
and regenerated,
not the successful
doing of a thing.

*"That My joy might remain in you,
and that your joy might be full."*
John 15:11

The joy of Jesus was the absolute self-surrender
and self-sacrifice of Himself to His Father,
the joy of doing that which the Father sent Him to do.

"Take My yoke upon you, and learn of Me."
Matthew 11:29

The fact that the peace and the light
and the joy of God are there is proof
that the burden is there too.

LOVE

"I have called you friends."
John 15:15

Love for God is not sentimental,
for the saint to love as God loves
is the most practical thing.

"Feed my sheep."
John 21:17

And Jesus has some
extraordinarily funny sheep,
some bedraggled, dirty sheep,
some awkward, butting sheep,
some sheep that have gone astray!

"Add to your brotherliness. . .love."
2 Peter 1:7

God's love to me is inexhaustible,
and I must love others from the bedrock
of God's love to me.

Love

"Charity suffereth long, and is kind. . . ."
1 Corinthians 13:4

Love is not premeditated, it is spontaneous,
i.e., it bursts up in extraordinary ways.

*"Nay, in all these things we are more than
conquerors through Him that loved us."*
Romans 8:37

The bedrock of
our Christian faith is the unmerited,
fathomless marvel of the love
of God exhibited on the Cross of Calvary,
a love we never can and never shall merit.

OBEDIENCE

"If ye love Me,
ye will keep
My commandments."
John 14:15 (RV)

Our Lord never insists
upon obedience;
He tells us very emphatically
what we ought to do,
but He never takes means
to make us do it.

"And he said, Who art Thou, Lord?"
Acts 9:5

A man is a slave for obeying unless
behind his obedience
there is a recognition of a holy God.

"By Myself have I sworn, saith the LORD,
for because thou hast done this thing. . .
that in blessing I will bless thee. . . ."
Genesis 22:16–17

There is no possibility of questioning
when God speaks if He speaks to His own nature in me;
prompt obedience
is the only result.

"Let us go into Judaea again.
His disciples say unto Him. . .
Goest thou thither again?"
John 11:7–8

Obey Him with glad reckless joy.

"I thank Thee, O Father. . .
because Thou hast hid these things
from the wise and prudent,
and hast revealed them unto babes."
Matthew 11:25

The tiniest fragment of obedience,
and heaven opens and the profoundest
truths of God are yours straight away.

ONENESS WITH GOD

"At that day ye shall ask in My name."
John 16:26

The idea of prayer is not in order to get answers from God;
prayer is perfect and complete oneness with God.

"Saul, Saul, why persecutest thou Me?"
Acts 26:14

All I do ought to be founded
on a perfect oneness with Him,
not on a self-willed determination to be godly.

"That they all may be one; as thou,
Father, art in me, and I in thee,
that they also may be one in us."
John 17:21

God will not leave us alone
until we are one with Him,
because Jesus has prayed that we may be.

"I do set my bow in the cloud,
and it shall be for a token of
a covenant between Me and the earth."
Genesis 9:13

All the great blessings of God are finished and complete,
but they are not mine until I enter into relationship with Him
on the basis of His covenant.

"But have renounced the
hidden things of dishonesty."
2 Corinthians 4:2

Many have gone back because
they are afraid of looking at things
from God's standpoint.

PATIENCE

"Be still, and know that I am God."
Psalm 46:10

One of the greatest strains in life
is the strain of waiting for God.

Patience

"Though it tarry, wait for it."
Habakkuk 2:3

Patience is not indifference;
patience conveys the idea of an immensely
strong rock withstanding all onslaughts.

"When Jesus had made an end of commanding
his twelve disciples, he departed thence
to teach and to preach in their cities."
Matthew 11:1

To wait is not to sit with folded hands,
but to learn to do what we are told.

PEACE

"Peace I leave with you,
My peace I give unto you."
John 14:27

Reflected peace is the proof
that you are
right with God because you
are at liberty
to turn your mind to Him.
If you are not right with God,
you can never turn your mind
anywhere but on yourself.

PRAYER

"But we trusted. . .and beside all this,
to-day is the third day. . . ."
Luke 24:21

The meaning of prayer is that we get hold of God,
not of the answer.

"Lord, that I may receive my sight."
Luke 18:41

If it is an impossibility,
it is the thing we have to ask. . . .
God will do the absolutely impossible.

"Pray without ceasing."
1 Thessalonians 5:17

God answers prayer in the best way,
not sometimes, but every time,
although the immediate manifestation of the answer
in the domain in which we want it
may not always follow.

*"We. . .beseech you also that ye receive
not the grace of God in vain."*
2 Corinthians 6:1

Prayer is the exercise of
drawing on the grace of God.

"Lord, teach us to pray."
Like 11:1

If we think of prayer as the breath in our lungs
and the blood from our hearts, we think rightly.
The blood flows ceaselessly,
and breathing continues ceaselessly;
we are not conscious of it, but it is always going on.

"At that day ye shall ask in My name."
John 16:26

When prayer seems to be unanswered, beware of trying
to fix the blame on someone else. . . .
You will find there is a reason which is a deep instruction
to you, not to anyone else.

*"Wherefore take unto you the whole armour of God. . .
praying always. . . ."*
Ephesians 6:13, 18

If you ask me to pray for you and I am not
complete in Christ, I may pray but it avails
nothing; but if I am complete in Christ my prayer prevails
all the time. Prayer is only effective when there is completeness–
"Wherefore take unto you the whole armour of God."

REDEMPTION

"When it pleased God. . .to reveal His Son in me."
Galatians 1:15–16

The moral miracle of Redemption is
that God can put into me a new disposition
whereby I can live a totally new life.

"But ye are. . .a royal priesthood."
1 Peter 2:9

Launch out in reckless belief that the Redemption
is complete, and then bother no more about
yourself, but begin to do as Jesus Christ said–
pray for the friend who comes to you at midnight,
pray for the saints, pray for all men.

"Wherefore, as by one man
sin entered into the world, and death by sin;
and so death passed upon all men,
for that all have sinned."
Romans 5:12

Sin is a thing I am born with and I cannot touch it;
God touches sin in Redemption.

REGENERATION

"And if thy right hand offend thee, cut it off, and cast it from thee:
for it is profitable for thee that one of thy members should perish,
and not that thy whole body should be cast into hell."
Matthew 5:30

When God alters a man by regeneration,
the characteristic of the life to begin with is
that it is maimed.

"Lord, that I may receive my sight."
Luke 18:41

The most impossible thing to you is that
you should be so identified with the Lord
that there is nothing of the old life left.
He will do it if you ask Him.

"Or what man is there of you,
whom if his son ask bread,
will he give him a stone?"
Matthew 7:9

I am a child of God only by regeneration. . . .

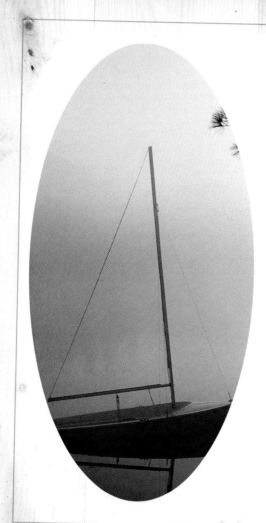

REPENTANCE

"For godly sorrow worketh
repentance to salvation."
2 Corinthians 7:10

The bedrock of Christianity
is repentance.

"I indeed baptize you with water. . .
but He. . .shall baptize you
with the Holy Ghost, and with fire."
Matthew 3:11

Repentance does not bring a sense of sin,
but a sense of unutterable unworthiness.

"For by one offering he hath perfected for ever
them that are sanctified."
Hebrews 10:14

Our repentance is merely the outcome of our
personal realization of the Atonement which
He has worked out for us.

RESURRECTION LIFE

"Ye must be born again."
John 3:7

To be born of God
means that I have
the supernatural power
of God to stop sinning.

"And Abraham built an altar. . .
and bound Isaac his son."
Genesis 22:9

God nowhere tells us to
give up things for the sake of giving them up.
He tells us to give them up for the sake of the
only thing worth having—viz., life with Himself.

"Only in the throne will I be greater than thou."
Genesis 41:40

I have to account to God for the way in which
I rule my body under His domination. . . .
Every saint can have his body
under absolute control for God.

Resurrection Life

"By this we believe. . . . Jesus answered,
Do ye now believe?"
John 16:30–31

Many a Christian worker has left Jesus Christ
alone and gone into work from a sense of duty,
or from a sense of need arising out
of his own particular discernment.
The reason for this is the absence of
the resurrection life of Jesus.

"All my fresh springs shall be in Thee."
Psalm 87:7 (PBV)

But as we bring every bit of our bodily life
into harmony with the new life which God
has put in us, He will exhibit in us the virtues
that were characteristic of the Lord Jesus.

SANCTIFICATION

"Walk while ye have the light,
lest darkness come upon you."
John 12:35

If you say you are sanctified, show it.
The experience must be so genuine
that it is shown in the life.

Sanctification

"This is the will of God,
even your sanctification."
1 Thessalonians 4:3

Am I willing to let Jesus
be made sanctification to me,
and to let the life of Jesus
be manifested in my mortal flesh?

"And the very God of peace sanctify you wholly."
1 Thessalonians 5:23

Sanctification means being made one with Jesus
so that the disposition that ruled Him will rule us. . . .
It will cost everything that is not of God in us.

"Abraham had two sons,
the one by a bondmaid,
the other by a freewoman."
Galatians 4:22

Sanctification means more than deliverance from sin,
it means the deliberate commitment of myself whom God has
saved to God, and that I do not care what it costs.

"And my speech and my preaching was not with enticing words
of man's wisdom, but in demonstration of the
Spirit and of power."
1 Corinthians 2:4

I have deliberately to give
my sanctified life to God for His service,
so that He can use me as His hands and His feet.

SERVICE

*"Building up yourselves
on your most holy faith."*
Jude 20

It is inbred in us
that we have to do
exceptional things
for God; but we have not.
We have to be exceptional
in the ordinary things. . . .

*"Who now rejoice in my sufferings for you,
and fill up that which is behind of the afflictions of Christ
in my flesh for His body's sake."*
Colossians 1:24

We must never choose
the scene of our own martyrdom.

*"Though the more abundantly I love you,
the less I be loved."*
2 Corinthians 12:15

His idea is that we serve Him
by being the servants of other men.
Jesus Christ out-socialists the socialists.

"Yea, and if I be offered upon the sacrifice
and service of your faith,
I joy, and rejoice with you all."
Philippians 2:17

Suppose God wants to teach you to say,
"I know how to be abased"–
are you ready to be offered up like that? Are you ready to be
not so much as a drop in a bucket. . . ?

"If I then, your Lord and Master, have washed your feet;
ye also ought to wash one another's feet."
John 13:14

The things that Jesus did were of the most menial
and commonplace order, and this is an indication that it takes
all God's power in me to do the most
commonplace things in His way.

SIMPLICITY

"The simplicity that is in Christ."
2 Corinthians 11:3

Simplicity is the secret of seeing things clearly.

"Have I been so long time with you,
and yet hast thou not known Me, Philip?"
John 14:9

It is opinions of our own which make us stupid,
when we are simple we are never stupid,
we discern all the time.

"And all things that are written by
the prophets concerning the Son of Man
shall be accomplished. . . . And they
understood none of these things."
Luke 18:31, 34

If we have a purpose of our own,
it destroys the simplicity and the leisureliness
which ought to characterize the children of God.

TRUST

*"Jesus did not commit
Himself unto them. . .
for He knew what
was in man."*
John 2:24–25

Never trust anything
but the grace
of God in yourself
or in anyone else.

"Be still, and know that I am God."
Psalm 46:10

The greatest fear a man has is not that he will be damned,
but that Jesus Christ will be worsted, that the things
He stood for—love and justice and forgiveness and kindness
among men—will not win out in the end. . . .
God is not going to be worsted.

"Lo, I come to do thy will, O God."
Hebrews 10:9

If our trust is placed in human beings,
we shall end in despairing of everyone.

UTMOST

*"Behold, as the eyes of servants look unto
the hand of their masters. . .
so our eyes wait upon the LORD our God."*
Psalm 123:2

We have to realize that no effort can be too high.

"While ye have light, believe in the light."
John 12:36

We must bring our commonplace life
up to the standard
revealed in the high hour.

"I was not disobedient unto the heavenly vision."
Acts 26:19

The only way to be obedient to the heavenly
vision is to give our utmost for God's highest,
and this can only be done by continually
and resolutely recalling the vision.

VISION

"Have mercy upon us,
O LORD, have mercy upon us:
for we are exceedingly
filled with contempt."
Psalm 123:3

It is extraordinary what
an enormous power
there is in simple things
to distract our attention
from God.

Track	Title	Time	© ℗
1	Here Is Love	2:02	(1)
2	Go (Into the World)	3:05	(2)
3	Time Is Too Short	2:40	(2)
4	Our Confidence Is in the Lord	5:01	(1)
5	To You Alone	2:17	(2)
6	O Sacred Head	2:06	(1)
7	We Are Here to Praise You	3:35	(1)
8	Lord, Lift Me Higher	2:42	(2)
9	No Weapon Formed Against Me	2:51	(2)
10	From Heaven You Came	3:34	(1)

TOTAL RUNNING TIME (29:58)

Copyright and Permissions
1–Kingsway Music LTD
2–Classic Fox Records LTD